Ronda Stevens

Twists N Turns
The Art
of
Wire Wrap Design

Ronda Stevens

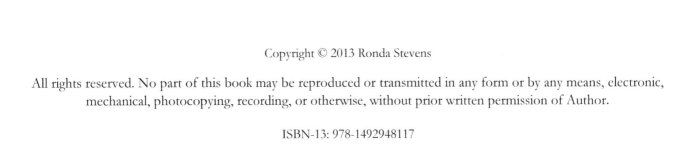

DEDICATION

This book is dedicated to my husband of 25 years, Ed Stevens. He has given me so much, but one of the most wonderful things is the confidence that he has shown in me. I would never have grown in this field if he wasn't there by my side, going to art shows, joining the lapidary club and even jumping in himself by taking classes in cutting and polishing cabochons and opals, as well as silversmith classes. He is truly my best friend and as he lovingly calls himself, my "CEIO". Ed, I couldn't have written this book without you. All my love.

CONTENTS

	Acknowledgments	**Page**
1	Introduction to Wire Wrap Basics	1
2	Ammonite Pendant	6
3	Interchangeable Cabochon Pendant	18
4	Tiffany Bracelet	27
5	Whimsical Weave Bracelet	34
6	Cabochon Ring	41
7	Channel Bracelet	48
8	Crystal Teardrop Pendant	55
9	Woven Bangle	62
10	Double Loop Cabochon Wrap	71

ACKNOWLEDGMENTS

I have a wonderful group of ladies who have taken my classes for years. When they heard of my plans to write a book, they volunteered to proofread it for me. I jumped on the offer. They are school teachers and jewelry artists; what better combination is there! Thank you, Gail and Toni. A special thanks to Pat and Jerry for hosting our wire wrapping classes in your homes.

My students are why I travel to dozens of cities, averaging 30 weekends a year. It's like seeing old friends when they stop by just to say hello or take another class. Their friendship and their joy in learning mean the world to me.

1

WIRE WRAPPING BASICS

Wire wrapping is an ancient art that involves making jewelry without solder. Wire is bent or folded to form jewelry from simple bangles to elaborate collars. Wire wrapped jewelry has taken on many forms throughout the ages, but traditional wire wrap designs are timeless. In my book, I'd like to offer you designs that use traditional wire wrapping techniques with a twist.

I have been teaching wire wrap design to beginning and intermediate level students for seven years. I find myself repeating certain things in every class, no matter what the project. I will include these little "good to know" items in boxes throughout the book.

This book is intended as a project book, and not a complete guide on wire wrapping tools, materials and techniques. There are many wonderful books on the market that cover all tools and wire available to the jewelry artist. I will list the tools and wire necessary to complete each project in this book. In this section, I will cover basic processes that are in almost all wire wrapping designs. I will repeat these processes in the first project, but in future projects, I will refer to the process, not a step-by-step for sake of brevity.

How to Straighten Wire

Grasp one end of the wire with flat-nose pliers. Run a polishing cloth with light pressure slowly down the length of the wire (Figure 1). If you apply too much pressure, the wire will only curve in the opposite direction.

Figure 1

How to Tape Wire

The proper way to tape wire may seem silly, but the correct way will hold your wire in the desired position and will make the removal of tape so much easier.

You do not want the sticky sides of your tape to touch or it will be very difficult to remove, and you may end up damaging your wire. Start the tape on the wire (Figure 2) and press firmly. Bring tape around so that your wires are touching, but not overlapping. It is only necessary to wrap the tape 2 or 3 times, keeping the wire flat as you wrap. Use the flat-nose pliers to press the tape flat and to ensure none of your wires have overlapped. Leave a ½" tail on your tape, and then fold it back on itself to make a handle for easy removal (Figure 3).

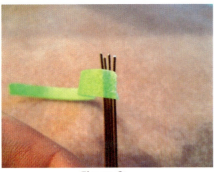

Figure 2

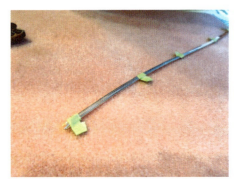

Figure 3

How to Wrap Using Half-Round Wire

Take half-round wire and determine the top and the bottom. The top is the domed side and the bottom is the flat side. The flat side must lie against the square wires each time you make a wrap. Do not twist the wire as you are wrapping, bend the wire around your group of square wires.

Use flat-nose pliers to make a hook and pull the end slightly to the right (to the left if you are left-handed). See Figures 4 – 6.

Figure 4

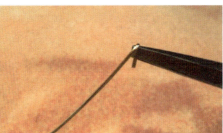

Figure 5

Figure 6

Place hooked wire on the wires to be wrapped. Use flat-nose pliers to hold the hook (Figure 7). Do not grasp the front of your half-round, only the hook. Begin wrapping the wire, being careful not to twist the wire as you wrap (Figure 8). Maintain a slight pressure on the wire as you wrap, and press each wrap gently with your pliers after they are made.

Figure 7

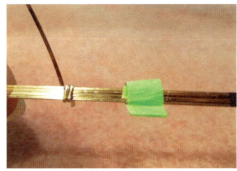

Figure 8

How to Trim Wire

ALWAYS WEAR EYE PROTECTION WHEN WORKING WITH WIRE.

When trimming any wire, it is extremely important to keep the wire covered. You can place your finger over the end of the cutter when trimming small pieces. Remember, you may be wearing eye protection, but those around you aren't. Those pieces of wire will travel quite far and can injure.

Trim half-round wire on the same side of the project every time. You don't want a finished piece of jewelry to have cut ends showing. Trim wire close to the edge (Figure 9) and use the tip of the chain-nose pliers to press the cut end down smooth.

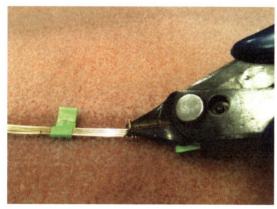

Figure 9

Creating Loops and Hinged Hooks for Bracelets

Loops: Slightly angle the 2 outer wires. Using round-nose pliers close to the end of the wire, make loops rolling over the top of the wire. (Figures 10 – 13).

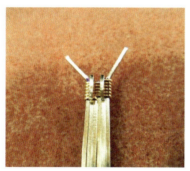

Figure 10

Figure 11

Figure 12

Figure 13

Hook: Take 3 inches of 20-gauge square half-hard wire; find the center (Figure 14). Using your chain-nose pliers at the tip, bend the wire in half. Use your pliers and continue bending this wire until both sides are flush against each other (Figure 15). Use the chain-nose pliers and turn the bent end up slightly (Figure 16). Place this bent end up in your round-nose pliers and roll the wires over to form a shepherd's hook (Figures 17 – 19). Measure from the top of the hook down the back straight wires ½" and mark (Figure 20). Place your flat-nose pliers over the hook and align the end of the pliers with that mark. Bend the wires out 45-degrees (Figure 21). Trim these wires to 3/8" past the bend. Use your round-nose pliers and make loops curving up to the hook on both wires (Figures 22 - 25).

Figure 14

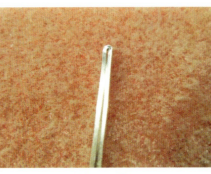

Figure 15

Figure 16

Figure 17

Figure 18

Figure 19

Figure 20

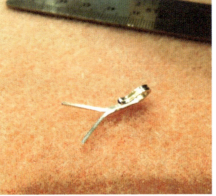

Figure 21

Figure 22

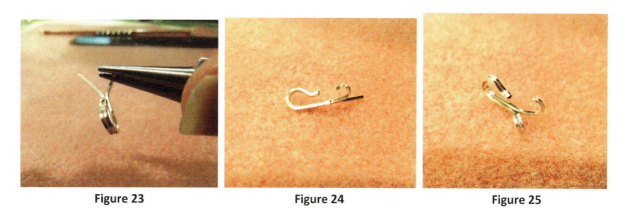

Figure 23 **Figure 24** **Figure 25**

Attach hook to bracelet loops. Gently close loops so that they hinge easily (Figure 43 on page 33).

2

WIRE WRAPPED AMMONITE PENDANT

Tools Required
Flush cutters
Flat-nose pliers
Chain-nose pliers
Round-nose pliers
Ruler
Marker
Tape
Polishing cloth

Materials Required
Ammonite
4 ft. of 21-gauge square dead-soft wire
1 ft. of 21-gauge half-round half-hard wire

Wire wrapped pendants are a must have in your wire wrapping projects. Learn to wrap unusual shapes and sizes to make your jewelry unique.

Step 1. Create Template

Use ¼" tape to create a template of your ammonite (Figure 1). Once the tape is in place, you will need to determine where to place the wraps. I use the wraps as a guide to determine the placement of the bends that act as prongs to hold your ammonite in place. Mark the tape where you will make your wraps. I usually mark a thin line on the tape for 3 to 4 wraps. However, if I need to cover a wider area, I will mark the tape with the beginning and end of the wrap area. Cut the tape flush at the top of your piece. Put your tape on the ruler as shown (Figure 2).

> Taping – Take the middle of the piece of tape and place it at the bottom of your piece. Roll the tape up the sides and let them meet at the top where the bail will be created.

Figure 1

Figure 2

Step 2. Prepare Wire

The measurement that was obtained using the tape is the baseline for the calculations. I usually add 5 to 6 inches to each piece of wire to allow enough for a nice bail and to enhance my piece. I always use a minimum of 3 wires when wrapping a pendant. One wire will be needed for front bends (prongs), a second wire is needed for back bends (prongs) and the third wire supports and frames the piece. If you have a thicker piece like I do with the ammonite, you can choose to use more than 3 wires. I'm going to use 4 in this project. I will cut four 10 inch pieces of 21-gauge square dead-soft wire. Straighten the wire using a polishing cloth (Figure 3). It is very important in wire wrapping to have your wires as straight as possible before wrapping (Figure 4).

Figure 3

Figure 4

> When straightening your wire, remember everything you do to a piece of wire hardens it. So take your time and don't overwork your wire.

Tape all four wires together starting at the end of the wire (Figure 5). The four wires need to lie side-by-side, touching each other. You should tape your wires every 2 inches (Figure 6).

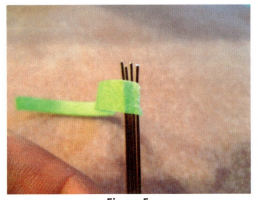
Figure 5

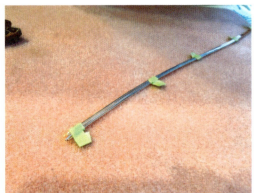
Figure 6

> When using tape, do not let the 2 sticky sides touch. Start the tape on your wire and wrap 2 or 3 times, then leave a ½" tail and fold it back on itself for ease of removal. Remember, tape is your friend.

Step 3. Transferring the Template to the Wire

Find the center of your taped wires (ours will be 5 inches since we cut all of our wires to 10 inches) and mark the wire (Figure 7). The template tape on my ruler was 4.5 inches, so the center of this will be 2.25 inches. Place an "X" on the template tape at 2.25 inches (Figure 8). Line these 2 measurements up, and then transfer every mark on the template tape to your group of wires. Also, mark your wire at each end of the template (Figure 9). If the center mark on your wire does not line up with any of the original marks made, you can now cover that mark with a piece of tape to avoid confusion during the next step.

Figure 7

Figure 8

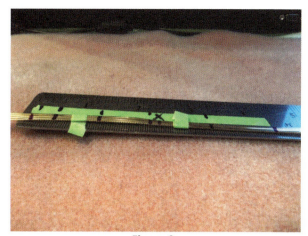

Figure 9

Ink marks may be removed from wire using acetone or fingernail polish remover.

Step 4. Begin Wrapping

Take half-round wire and determine the top and the bottom. The top is the domed side and the bottom is the flat side. The flat side must lie against the square wires each time you make a wrap. Do not twist the wire as you are wrapping; bend the wire around your group of square wires.

You will make at least 3 wraps at each mark you transferred from your template, except the marks made referencing the end of the template tape. There will be more than 3 wraps at the flat section of the ammonite. Refer back to Figure 1; wraps will be made to completely fill the flat area of the ammonite.

Using flat-nose pliers, make a hook and pull end slightly to the right (to the left if you are left-handed). See Figures 10, 11, and 12.

Figure 10

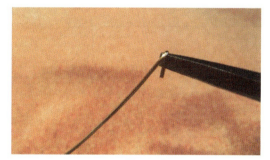

Figure 11

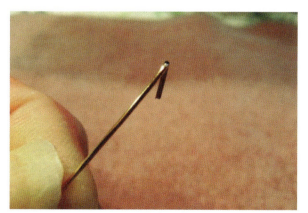

Figure 12

Begin wrapping at the marks. Use your flat-nose pliers to hold the back side of the hook. This will allow you to wrap the wire and not wrap over the jaws of the pliers (Figures 13 and 14). Press with the pliers, each wrap as it is made.

Figure 13

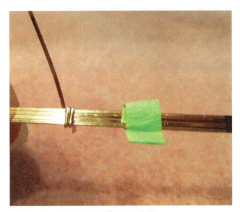
Figure 14

Continue wrapping at each mark. Remember, you will need to make numerous wraps at the marks that represent the straight section of your ammonite (Figure 15). Since ammonites vary in size, the number of wraps will also vary. Trim all wires on the same side, the side that touches the ammonite. The wires should be trimmed just enough to fold over the group of square wires (Figure 16). You do not want to feel the cut ends if you run your fingers down the side of the wires.

Figure 15

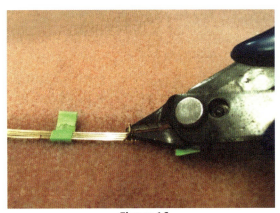
Figure 16

Step 5. Begin Shaping the Frame

Remove all tape from the square wire except for the 2 pieces on each end. Arrange the wire so that the cut ends of the wraps are next to the ammonite. Begin with the flat section of the ammonite. Make a sharp bend past the long set of wraps (Figure 17), then start gradually shaping around the ammonite. Once at the top, bend the wire out slightly and bring it flat against the other side (Figure 18).

Figure 17

Figure 18

> To get a good fit around the top of a wire wrapped pendant, bend the wires out slightly, where the marks were made indicating the end of the template tape. This will allow the wires to lie side-by-side.

Once the frame has a good fit, tape all 8 wires together (Figure 19). Bend the remaining 8 inches of 21-gauge square wire in half using the tip of your chain-nose pliers (Figure 20).

Figure 19

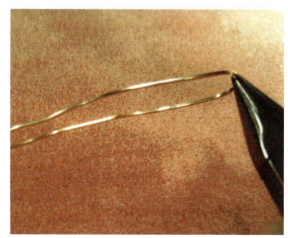

Figure 20

Place this wire from the back side of your frame to the front and squeeze gently; the wires will naturally cross (Figure 21). Now bring each wire back around to the back, keeping them stacked above and below (Figure 22). This will keep the wires neat. Remove all tape.

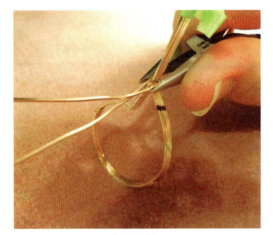

Figure 21

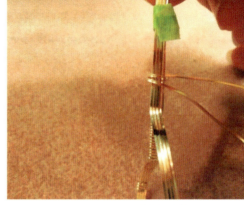

Figure 22

> When cutting wire of any type, always cover your cutter with your hand. Even if wearing glasses, you don't want those sharp pieces of wire hurting anyone else in the family.

Step 6. Preparing the Frame

You will begin forming the bends that will capture the ammonite and hold it securely in the frame. Using flat-nose pliers, working on the front side of the frame, grasp the front wire next to the bottom wrap (Figure 23). Turn your pliers toward the center of the frame (Figure 24). This will bend the front wire only. Next, grasp the front wire on the other side of the wrap (Figure 25). Continue bending front wires as shown in Figures 26 and 27. I like the decorative look of bending the 2nd wire down also (Figure 28).

Figure 23

Figure 24

Figure 25

Figure 26

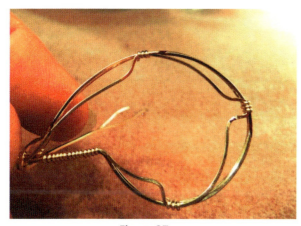
Figure 27

Figure 28

Step 7. Setting the Ammonite
Place the ammonite in the frame, face down (Figure 29). Grasp the back wire at the bottom and bring those wires over the back of the ammonite (Figure 30).

Figure 29

Figure 30

Repeat this process on the remaining wires (Figure 31).

Figure 31

Step 8. Form the Bail

Separate the wires into groups. The bail wires are 2 wires at the center front. Decorative wires are the remaining frame wires divided into 2 groups, half on each side. Then you have the back wires that are holding all of the wires securely (Figure 32).

Figure 32

Separate the back wires so that you can form the bail. The bail wires will lie down the back of the ammonite between the two back wires. Form your bail over something round that will provide you with the desired bail size. Lay the 2 front wires over the object to form the bail (Figure 33). Once formed, take chain-nose pliers and pinch the bail wires close to the ammonite in the back (Figure 34). The bail needs to be secured. You will use the back wires to wrap around the bail. Refer back to Figure 22 on page 12, to see how the wires are stacked. You will only wrap each wire around once. You will continue stacking the back wires as you wrap around the bail. You will have to hold one of the back wires down when making the first wrap, or they will shift (Figure 35). Using chain-nose pliers, press the wrapped wires from the front of the bail to flatten them in place (Figure 36).

Figure 33

Figure 34

Figure 35

Figure 36

Step 9. Enhance your Pendant

You choose how to enhance, decorate, and embellish your piece. Draping is one of my favorite techniques.

Draping: I allow the wire to bend and drape over the piece. I do not use tools for this. Simply grasp the ends of the wire, bring the wires across the piece and see where they look best (Figure 37). I then hold the wires in place and fold them to the back (Figure 38). I trim the ends (Figure 39) and secure them to one of the back wires (Figure 40). Always do this neatly. You want the back to look as neat as the front.

Figure 37

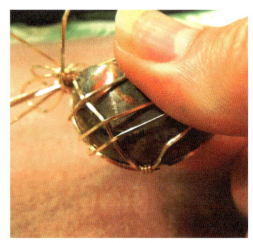

Figure 38

Figure 39

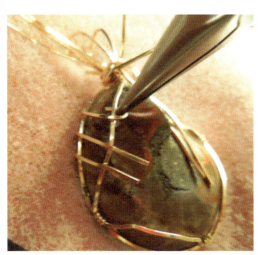

Figure 40

I drape the second set of wires, trim and secure them to the first set of wires that I draped (Figure 41). I trim the back wires and tuck the cut ends between the ammonite and the bail wraps. I then scroll the long bail wires on the back (Figure 42).

Figure 41

Figure 42

Completed Ammonite Pendant

3

INTERCHANGEABLE CABOCHON PENDANT

Tools Required
Flush cutters
Flat-nose pliers
Chain-nose pliers
Round-nose pliers
3-step pliers
Ruler
Marker
Pin vise
Tape
Polishing cloth

Materials Required
30 x 40mm cabochon
3 ft. of 21-gauge square dead-soft wire
2 ft. of 20-gauge half-round half-hard wire
5 in. of 18-gauge round half-hard wire
3 in. of 20-gauge round half-hard wire
3 in. of 26-gauge round dead-soft wire
Small bead or crystal of choice

So many stones and one interchangeable frame! I designed this pendant to hold a standard 30 x 40mm cabochon. The secret is the hinge. Open, pop the cabochon out and slip a different one in.

Step 1. Preparing the Wire

Cut the 21-gauge square wire into three 10 inch lengths and straighten.

Find the center of 1 piece and mark it (Figure 1). Place your round-nose pliers about ¼" from the tips of the pliers on the mark that you made and bend the wire over the pliers (Figure 2). Mark your wire again at 1/8" from the top of the bend (Figure 3). Using your chain-nose pliers, grasp the wire at the mark (Figure 4) and make a sharp 90-degree bend out; repeat on the other side (Figure 5). Align your 3 wires with the looped wire on the outside and vertical (Figure 6). Tape wires.

Figure 1

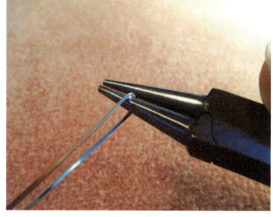

Figure 2

Figure 3

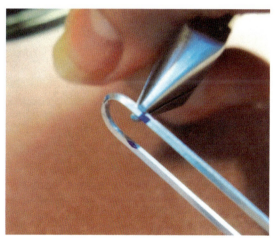

Figure 4

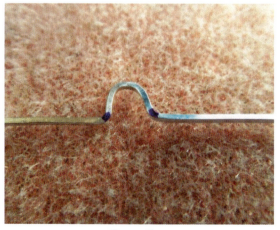

Figure 5

Figure 6

Step 2. Wrapping Your Wire

In Project 1, we created a template to determine where the wraps would be placed on the square wires. Since this pattern is for a specific size stone, we do not have to do this. With 20-gauge half-round wire, you will make 3 wraps on each side of the loop created in the previous step. You will then make 4 wraps, 1 inch past the first sets (Figure 7). Make sure you keep your cut ends on the underside. The side with the loop is the finished side.

Figure 7

Step 3. Shaping the Frame

Place the wire directly below the cabochon, making sure the looped wire is at the back (Figure 8). Begin shaping it around the sides (Figure 9).

Figure 8

Figure 9

Once the basic shape is achieved, secure the wire around the cabochon with tape, and gently bend the wires at the top so that they lie close together (Figure 10). Begin manipulating the top wires so that they lie flat at the top of the frame (Figure 11). It does not take much pressure to do this since we are using dead-soft wire. A gentle twisting motion will bring the wires together at the top. Once together, tape them about 1 inch from the cabochon. Using 18 inches of half-round wire, begin wrapping close to the cabochon, moving toward the cut ends (Figure 12). You will have to pull tightly on the first 2 wraps to get all 6 wires side-by-side. It is extremely important that you use flat-nose pliers as you make your wraps. Press each wrap as you go. This will ensure that your base wires do not bunch as you're wrapping. Continue wrapping until you have 1 inch of wraps (Figure 13). **DO NOT CUT** the half-round wire.

Figure 10

Figure 11

Figure 12

Figure 13

Step 4. Form the Bail

I like to bend my wrapped wires over a pen to form the bail (Figure 14). Bend the wires toward the back of the pendant. Once the basic shape is made (Figure 15), remove the pen and take the flat-nose pliers and bring the bail wires closer to the frame (Figure 16). Remove all tape and remove cabochon. Wrap the remaining half-round wire completely around the bail at least three times, then wrap it around the loose bail wires to secure it (Figure 17). Trim half-round wire. You have 6 wires hanging down the back of the frame. Bring the middle 2 through the frame and let them stay at the front (Figure 18). They will be used later.

Figure 14

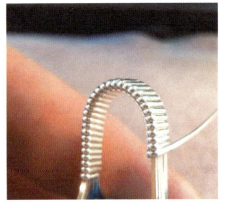

Figure 15

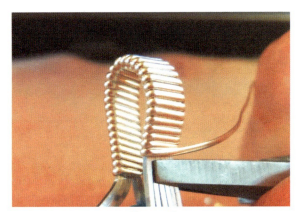

Figure 16

Figure 17

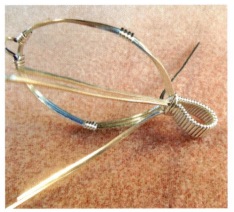

Figure 18

Step 5. Prepare the Frame to Receive the Hinge

Trim the remaining 4 wires to ½" past the wraps (Figure 19). Using the smallest step on 3-step pliers, roll those wires toward the frame (Figure 20). Do not close the loops completely, you will need to attach your hinged wire next. The frame should now look like this (Figure 21).

Figure 19

Figure 20

Figure 21

Step 6. Prepare the Hinge

Take the 5 inch piece of 18-gauge round half-hard wire, find the center and mark it (Figure 22). Using the tip of the round-nose pliers, bend the wire in half (Figure 23). Test the fit on the bottom loop of the frame (Figure 24).

Figure 22

Figure 23

Figure 24

Mark the wire ¼" from the bend (Figure 25). Take your flat-nose pliers and make a 90-degree bend at that mark (Figures 26 and 27). While still holding the tip of the wire, separate the wires (Figure 28). Use your fingers to round them roughly to the shape of your cabochon (Figure 29). Using the 1st step on the 3-step pliers, roll each end toward the center (Figure 30). Make sure the bend at the other end is facing the frame and attach these loops to the frame loops made earlier (Figure 31). Once attached, close the frame loops completely. If any adjustment is required to fit the hinged loop into the frame loop, make the sides of the hinged wire rounder or straighter. This will lengthen or shorten it.

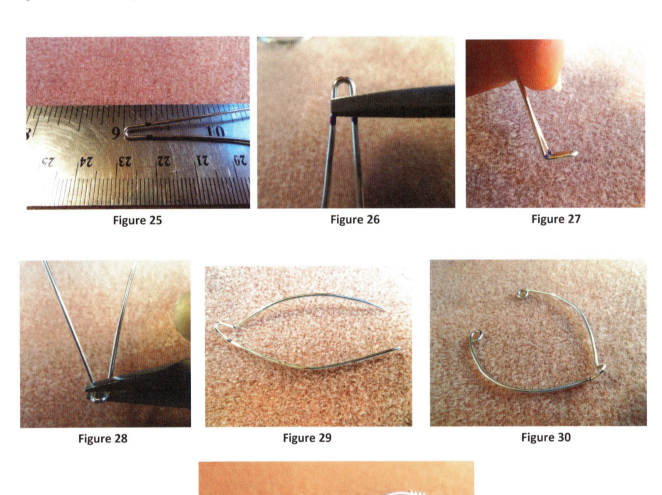

figure 25 **Figure 26** **Figure 27**

Figure 28 **Figure 29** **Figure 30**

Figure 31

Step 7. Finish the Frame

Make bends in your wire (Figure 32) to support the front of the cabochon. Twist the remaining wires with a pin vise, if desired; then scroll them at the front of the cabochon (Figures 33 – 35).

Figure 32

Figure 33

Figure 34

Figure 35

Put Cabochon into frame. Bend back wires just slightly over the back of the cabochon. It will be easy to pop the cabochon out, but these slight bends will assist in holding the cabochon in place.

Step 8. Create the Lock

Use 3 inches of 20-gauge round half-hard wire to form a hook that will secure the cabochon in the frame. Start by bending the end of the wire very tightly (Figure 36). Then form a hook using your round-nose pliers (Figures 37 and 38).

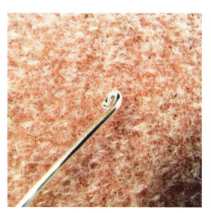

Figure 36

Figure 37

Figure 38

Test the fit into the frame loop (Figure 39). Make a wrapped loop on the end (Figure 40). You can use the 26 gauge wire to attach beads or stones as embellishments to the lock.

Figure 39

Figure 40

Completed Interchangeable Pendant

4

TIFFANY BRACELET

Tools Required
Flush cutters
Flat-nose pliers
Chain-nose pliers
Round-nose pliers
Ruler
Marker
Tape
Polishing cloth

Materials Required
For a 7 inch bracelet
44 in. of 20-gauge square half-hard wire
2.5 ft. of 20-gauge half-round half-hard wire
2 in. Tiffany style Swarovski Cup Chain 4mm

A Touch of Elegance in your Wire Wrapped Jewelry

Cup Chain Source Bead-N- Sisters
Susansudnik@aol.com

Step 1. Prepare Wire

Cut square wire into the following lengths:
- 2 14 inch pieces
- 2 6.5 inch pieces

Use the polishing cloth and straighten all wires.
Find the center of both 14 inch pieces and mark them (Figure 1).

Take one of the wires and make a mark at ¼" from the left side of center and another mark at 3/8" on the right side of center (Figure 2). Use the flat-nose pliers to grasp the wire at the left mark (Figure 3) and bend the wire at a 45-degree angle (Figure 4), repeat on the right mark (Figures 5 and 6). Grasp wire in your round-nose pliers, near the back at the largest part of the pliers. Keep the wire in the pliers with the bends up. Bring both sides down around your round-nose pliers. (Figures 7 and 8). You have just formed the outer keyhole.

Figure 1

Figure 2

Figure 3

Figure 4

Figure 5

Figure 6

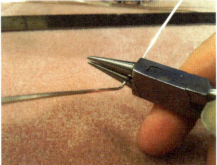

Figure 7

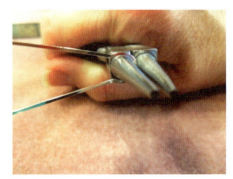

Figure 8

You will repeat the steps on the second wire, but to make it **smaller**, both marks will be **at ¼" on both the right and left side**. You will also use the **smaller part** of the round-nose pliers, close to the center (Figure 9).
These "keyholes" should lay one inside the other (Figure 10) with enough room to lay your 2 pieces of 6.5 inch wire inside (Figure 11). This is the eye of the bracelet. Tape about 1" from the eye.

Figure 9

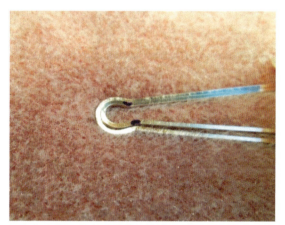

Figure 10

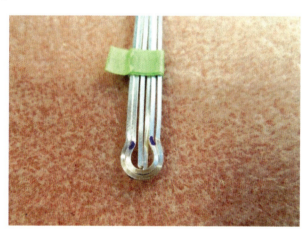

Figure 11

Step 2. Secure the Ends

Make 6 wraps at the eye end of the wire (Figure 12). Secure inner wires within the eye by bending them over the wraps, ensuring they are bent over the cut ends of the wraps (Figures 13 and 14).

Figure 12

Figure 13

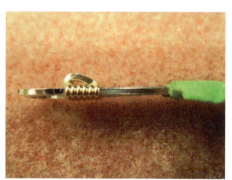

Figure 14

Move to the opposite end of the wire. Tape about 1" from the end. The 2 inner wires should be shorter than the 4 outer wires. Mark outer wires 3/8" from the end (Figure 15). Trim the 2 inner wires even with this mark. Make 6 wraps at this mark, wrapping toward the center. Bend the inner long wires over the wraps, just as was done on the opposite end (Figures 16 and 17). These wires will need to be trimmed before pressing down completely.

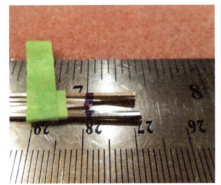
Figure15

Figure 16

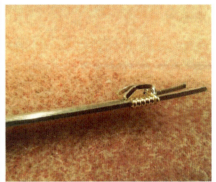
Figure 17

Slightly angle the 2 outer wires (Figure 18).These will be formed into loops that will accept the hook later. Using round-nose pliers close to the end, make loops rolling over the top of the wire (Figures 19 – 21).

Figure 18

Figure 19

Figure 20

Figure 21

Step 3. Make Wraps

Find the center between the 2 sets of wraps and mark (Figure 22). Take the 2 inch cup chain, which equals 7 crystals, and place the middle crystal on the mark at the middle of the bracelet (Figure 23). Tape the 2 end crystals securely to your wire (Figure 24). Be sure to pull them tight so that it will be easy to wrap between them. Measure 14 inches of half-round wire and bend in half. Starting in the middle of your cup chain, begin wrapping (Figure 25). You will make 2 wraps between each crystal. You may need to use the chain-nose pliers to press the wire securely between each. When making the transition between each crystal, angle the half-round on the back side, and start the wrap at the front as straight as possible (Figure 26). Continue wrapping until you have reached the last crystal (Figure 27). Make 5 wraps on the outside of the cup chain (Figure 28). Find the center between the last wraps on the cup chain and the end of the bracelet, and mark both sides. Make 4 wraps at these marks (Figures 29 and 30).

figure 22

Figure 23

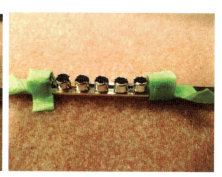
Figure 24

Figure 25

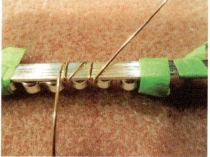
Figure 26

Figure 27

Figure 28

Figure 29

Figure 30

Step 4. Make the Hook

Take 3 inches of 20-gauge square half-hard wire; find the center (Figure 31). Using your chain-nose pliers at the tip, bend the wire in half. Use your pliers and continue bending this wire until both sides are flush against each other (Figure 32). Use the chain-nose pliers and turn the bent end up slightly (Figure 33). Place this bent end up in your round-nose pliers and roll the wires over to form a shepherds hook (Figures 34 – 36). Measure from the top of the hook down the back straight wires ½" and mark (Figure 37). Place your flat-nose pliers over the hook and align the end of the pliers with that mark. Bend the wires out 45-degrees (Figure 38). Trim these wires to 3/8" past the bend. Use your round-nose pliers and make loops curving up to the hook on both wires (Figures 39 - 42).

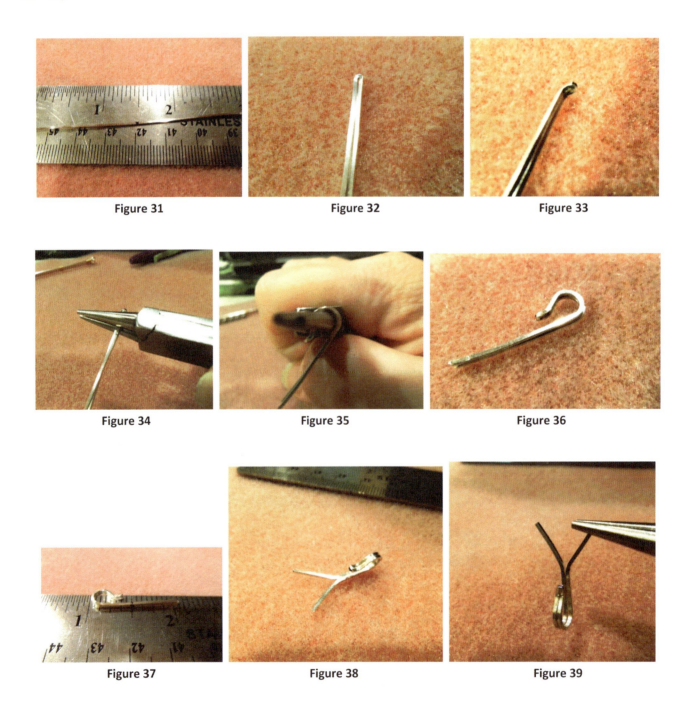

Figure 31 — Figure 32 — Figure 33

Figure 34 — Figure 35 — Figure 36

Figure 37 — Figure 38 — Figure 39

Figure 40

Figure 41

Figure 42

Attach hook to bracelet. Gently close loops so that they hinge easily (Figure 43). Shape bracelet using a bracelet mandrel.

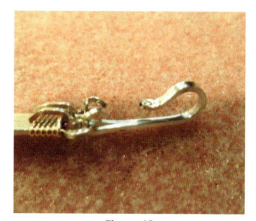
Figure 43

Completed Tiffany Bracelet

5

WHIMSICAL WEAVE BRACELET

Braided Silver Wire, Beads and a Touch of Whimsy

Tools Required		Materials Required
C – clamp	Tape	4 ft. of 18-gauge round dead-soft wire
Round-nose pliers	Ruler	**12 to 15 beads of choice
Flat-nose pliers	Polishing cloth	
Chain-nose pliers	Marker	
Flush cutters		

Make sure your beads fit on 18 gauge wire before starting.

Step 1. Prepare the Wire

Cut two 22 inch pieces of 18-gauge wire and straighten. Find the center of both and mark (Figure 1). Take one of the wires in your round-nose pliers near the center of the pliers and bend in half (Figures 2 and 3). Keep the pliers slightly open and roll the pliers in your hand (Figure 4). This will cause the wire below the loop to be bent in. Repeat on other side (Figure 5). You may need to repeat this to get the bottom wires to line up directly below the loop (Figure 6). **The pliers must be kept open or the bends will be removed each time you go to the other side.

figure 1

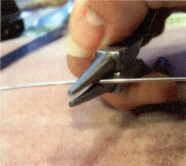

Figure 2

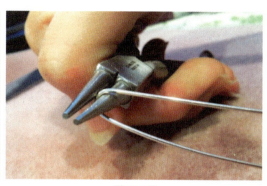

Figure 3

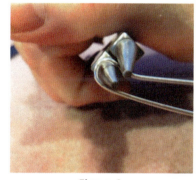

Figure 4

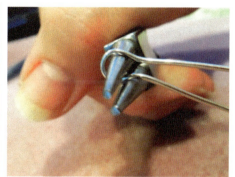

Figure 5

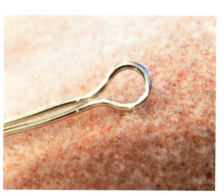

Figure 6

Take the 2nd 22 inch wire and using your flat-nose pliers, bend the wire in half (Figures 7 and 8).

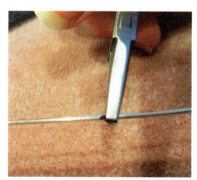

Figure 7

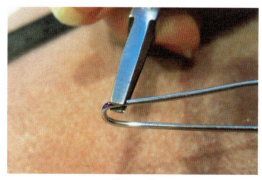

Figure 8

Take the wire that is bent in half and place it over the looped wire (Figure 9). Hold the top part of the bent wire with your pliers (Figure 10). Bring the bottom wire up and over the looped wire (Figure 11). You will have to pull tightly since this is 18-gauge wire. Use the flat-nose pliers to press the wraps (Figure 12). Use tape and cover the loop and wrap that you just made (Figure 13). We will be using a C-clamp to hold the wire to the work surface and this will keep the wire from being scratched. Use a C-clamp that will accommodate the thickness of your work surface. Clamp the wire to the table surface, ensuring that all wires are at the edge of the table (Figure 14).

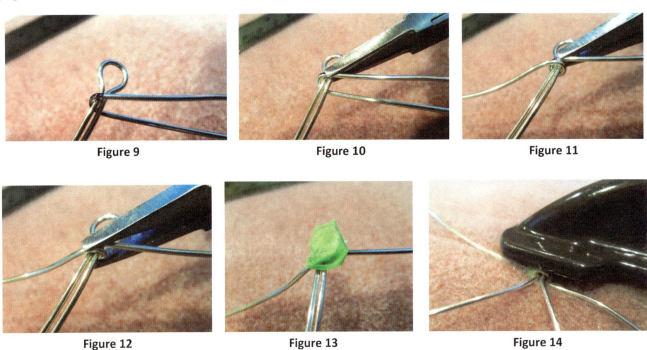

Figure 9   Figure 10   Figure 11

Figure 12   Figure 13   Figure 14

Step 2. Braiding

The first 2 bends are made simply to get the wires into a position to start braiding. You will make them tight so that they lie right against the eye of your bracelet. Take the far left wire and bend it to the back, out of your way. You will be working with 3 wires only for now. So when instructed to bring the left wire over, that means the left of the 3 wires. Bring the left wire to the center (Figure 15). Bring the right wire to the center (Figure 16).

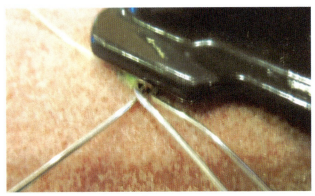

Figure 15

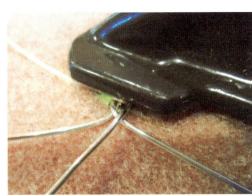

Figure 16

Add a bead to the left wire (Figure 17)

Figure 17

The length of your bracelet will depend on the size bead that you choose to use. For a 6.5 inch wrist, a 7 inch bracelet is comfortable. When adding beads, you have to consider the size of the beads. I used 6mm beads in this bracelet. So when measuring the bracelet on a ruler, I went to 7.5 inches to achieve my desired finished 7 inch bracelet. Don't forget to include the closures on your bracelet. The total length of the hook and eye in this project is 1 inch; so I only braided 6.5 inches.

A. Bring left wire with bead to the center. Make sure the bead slips over the center wire (Figure 18).

Figure 18

B. Bring right wire to the center, below the bead (Figure 19).

Figure 19

C. Bring left wire to center, below the bead (Figure 20).

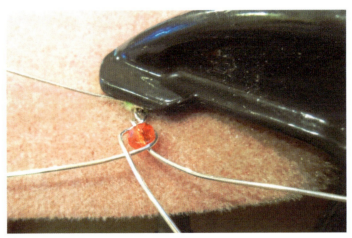

Figure 20

D. Bring right wire to center (Figure 21). This positions the wires perfectly to add a new bead (Figure 22).

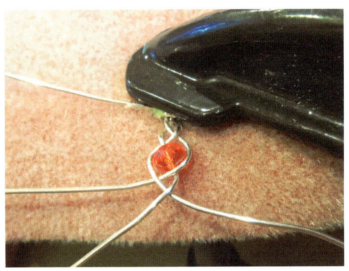

Figure 21

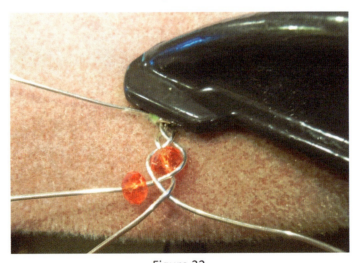

Figure 22

Repeat A through D until desired length (Figure 23). Now you will pick up the 4th wire and begin wrapping it randomly around the braid (Figure 24). Do not wrap too tightly, and don't try to be exact. This is the whimsical part of the bracelet.

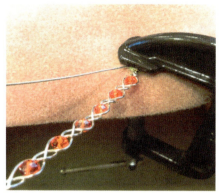
Figure 23

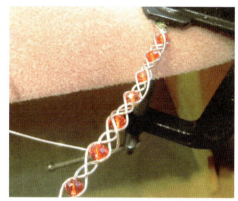
Figure 24

Bring the 4th wire to the end (Figure 25) and wrap it snugly around all 3 braided wires (Figure 26).

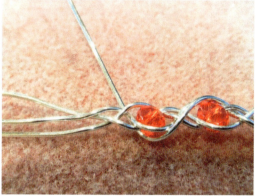
Figure 25

Figure 26

Trim wire on back (Figure 27). Press cut end down with chain-nose pliers (Figure 28). Trim middle wire to ¼" past the wrapped wire (Figure 29).

Figure 27

Figure 28

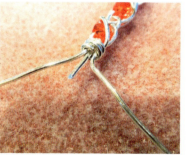
Figure 29

Fold the middle wire over the wrapped wire, keeping all cut ends on the same side of bracelet (Figure 30). Trim outer wires to 3/8" past wraps (Figure 31). Form loops, rolling both toward center (Figure 32).

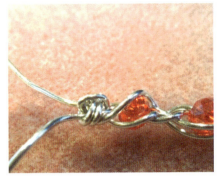
Figure 30

Figure 31

Figure 32

Make hook using 3 inches of 18-gauge round dead-soft wire (Figure 33). See page 4 for step by step instructions. Attach hook to bracelet (Figure 34). Form bracelet with hands or over a bracelet mandrel.

Figure 33

Figure 34

Completed Whimsical Weave Bracelet

6

CABOCHON RING

Tools Required

Flush cutters
Flat-nose pliers
Chain-nose pliers
Ruler
Pin vise
Ring Mandrel
Marker
Tape
Polishing cloth
Super Glue

Material Required

Oval cabochon of choice
32 in. of 21-gauge square dead- soft wire
8 in. of 22-gauge half-round

Nature Captured

Step 1. Prepare the Wire and Wrap Ring Shank.

Cut four 8 inch pieces of 21-gauge square dead-soft wire and straighten. Tape wires together, side-by-side at the center (Figure 1). Add 2 more pieces of tape close to each end. Mark wire at 3 inches and 5 inches. Use half-round wire, make 3 wraps at each mark (Figure 2). **Important Note:** These wraps must be moveable; **do not tighten.** Go ahead and move them closer to the center now.

Wrap wire around ring mandrel at desired ring size ensuring that you are at the center of the wire (Figure 3). The cut ends of the wraps must be on the outside. These will not show on the finished ring. Let the wires bypass each other and squeeze tightly. Make a mark across both sides (Figure 4).

Figure 1

Figure 2

Figure 3

Figure 4

Step 2. Form Ring Base

Slip the wire off the mandrel. Gently straighten the wires into a "U" (Figure 5). Remove the tape from the end. Leave the tape at the middle mark. Separate the 4 wires slightly. Slip your flat-nose pliers from the inside of the "U" and grasp 2 wires side-by-side (Figure 6). You will use the mark as your guide, but do not get exactly on the mark. You should be about 1/16" away. Grasp the wires with your fingers close to the tip of the pliers and bend both out 90-degrees at the same time (Figure 7). Repeat on other 2. Move the wrapping wire up and tighten (Figure 8). Repeat on other side. Place ring on mandrel and ensure that your size is still correct (Figure 9).

Figure 5

Figure 6

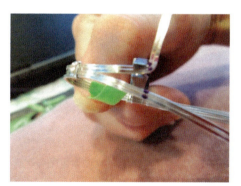

Figure 7

Figure 8

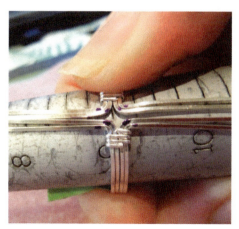

Figure 9

Tape the wire about 1 inch from the center (Figure 10). You will lay your cabochon on the wire to determine where your wraps will be placed (Figure 11). Mark the wires (Figure 12). Wrap the wire 3 times at each mark, keeping the cut ends on the top of the wire (Figure 13). Make 2 more sets of wraps at the center, also keeping the cut ends on the outside (Figure 14).

Figure 10

Figure 11

Figure 12

Figure 13

Figure 14

We will be using Super Glue to temporarily hold our cabochon in place so that the wire bends can be made evenly. If the cabochon has a polished back, use a file and rough it up slightly. Use the flat nose pliers to flatten the area where the cabochon will sit on the frame. Apply glue to the cabochon and sit your wire frame on it (Figure 15). Make sure it is lined up properly, then let it dry. Once dry, you can turn it over and begin work (Figure 16).

Figure 15

Figure 16

Step 3. Secure Cabochon

Remove tape on straight wire, leaving the tape on the ring shank. Separate the wires on each end of the cabochon (Figure 17). If you'd like to twist the center wires with a pin vise, now is the time to do it (Figure 18). The ring pictured has the center wires twisted.

Figure 17

Figure 18

Next, begin draping the wire over the cabochon. It is important to keep your wires over the top of the cabochon as you're working. It's very easy to start wrapping the wire around the shank too tightly and pull the wire off the side of the cabochon. Remember the glue will break loose, and the wire is what is necessary to hold your stone in place. Drape the outer wires over the ring shank. I like to line up the "X" formed from the wires with the ring shank. (Figure 19) I will use my finger to hold the wire in place as I start working the ends through the shank (Figure 20). Use your chain-nose pliers to gently manipulate your wires as they circle the shank. Make the opening as small as possible, without pulling your wires off the stone (Figure 21).

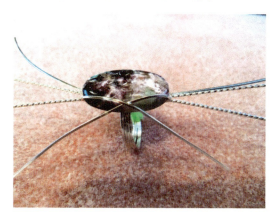
Figure 19

Figure 20

Figure 21

Trim wires about ¼" past the shank (Figure 22). Use the chain-nose pliers to lay them into the opening (Figure 23). Both wires should fit neatly on the shank with the cut ends facing the stone (Figure 24). Repeat on other side (Figure 25).

Figure 22

Figure 23

Figure 24

Figure 25

Twisting square wire with a pin vise gives a nice look to any wire wrapped project. It is best to use dead soft wire. Half-hard wire tends to twist unevenly. However, if you need half-hard in your project, twist your square dead-soft wire and now you have the hardness that you require.

Also remember that a pin vise is hollow. The wire that goes into a pin vise doesn't twist. This can come in handy for certain projects.

So use a pin vise to add a little twist to your next piece of jewelry.

Next you will drape the inner wires. This is done exactly the same as the previous wires, just make sure you lay them more toward the center of the stone (Figure 26). You will wrap these on the outside of the wires already on the shank (Figure 27). Leave the wires long until you make sure the wires lie exactly as you want them (Figure 28). Trim and press the last 2 wires with your chain-nose pliers into the circle (Figure 29). Put ring on ring mandrel and using a rawhide mallet, hammer the shank (Figure 30). This will round out the shank and also tighten the wires that have been wrapped within the ring shank.

Figure 26

Figure 27

Figure 28

Figure 29

Figure 30

Completed Cabochon Ring

7

CHANNEL BRACELET

Tools Required
Flush cutters
Flat-nose pliers
Chain-nose pliers
Round-nose pliers
3-step pliers
Ruler
Marker
Tape
Polishing Cloth

Materials Required
3x6mm Czechmates Brick beads 25 to 30 beads
Small Spacer beads if desired
4.5 ft. 20-gauge square half-hard wire
16 in. 22-gauge square half-hard wire
40 in. 20 gauge half-round half- hard wire

A NEW STYLE FOR A CLASSIC WIRE WRAP DESIGN

The beauty of this channel bracelet is that it is very easy to adjust, so that a variety of beads fits within the channel. Find the width of your bead and you have determined the width of your channel. Of course, if the bead is very wide, the measurements of the square wire will need to be increased. Just add a few inches and give it a try.

Step 1. Prepare Your Wire

Cut three 16 inch pieces of 20-gauge square wire and straighten.

Cut two 8 inch pieces of 22-gauge square wire and straighten.

Mark the three 16 inch pieces of wire at 7 inches, 8 inches and 9 inches. Tape them together only at the 7 inch and the 9 inch marks (Figure 1).

Lay your bead against the 8 inch mark so that you can determine how many wraps you will need to make to accommodate the width of your bead (Figure 2). Mark your wire, then wrap (Figures 3 and 4).

Figure 1

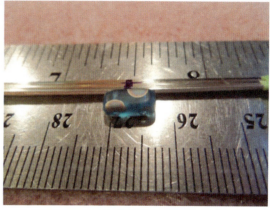

Figure 2

Figure 3

Figure 4

Grasp the wraps that you just made on the edge with your flat-nose pliers (Figure 5). Bend the side down at a 90-degree bend (Figure 6). If you keep your fingers on the wire next to the pliers, you'll have more control of your wire. Repeat on other side.

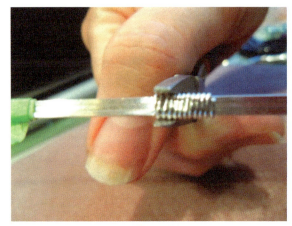
Figure 5

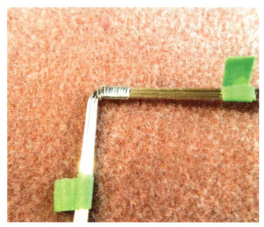
Figure 6

Step 2. Start Adding Beads

Take the two 8 inch pieces of wire and add the first set of beads. The bead sets should be no larger than ½". Shown is 3 beads with small spacer beads. If the area is too long between wraps, the bracelet will not bend properly.

Tape the beads in place (Figure 7). This will be done continually throughout this bracelet. This process keeps the channel at the correct width while wrapping. Mark your wire ½" from finished end of the bracelet. Make 4 wraps at the mark, wrapping toward the finished end. Trim half-round wires so that they end on the outer square wires (Figure 8).

Figure 7

Figure 8

Secure the bead wires by looping the ends over the back of the wrap wires with your chain-nose pliers (Figure 9). Remove tape, push set of beads into place (Figure 10). Add another set of beads and tape them in place leaving a ½" gap between the 2 sets (Figure 11). Make 3 wraps between each set of beads (Figure 12). Continue adding beads and wraps until you have reached the desired length, which is ¾" less than the finished length of 7 inches.

Figure 9

Figure 10

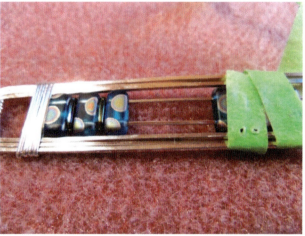

Figure 11

Figure 12

Step 3. Finishing the Bracelet

Make 4 wraps after the last set of beads (Figure 13). Trim inner wires to ¼" past wraps (Figure 14). Use chain-nose pliers to form loops over the wrapped wires (Figure 15). Mark remaining wires ½" past the wraps (Figure 16). Trim wires at the mark and bend wires up slightly (Figure 17). Use 2nd step on 3-step pliers and form loops, rolling to the back (Figure 18).

Figure 13

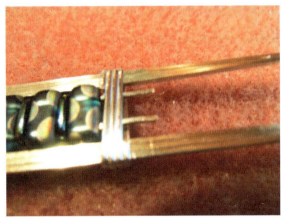

Figure 14

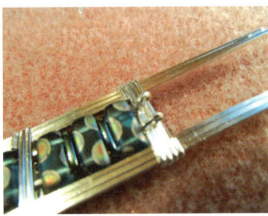

Figure 15

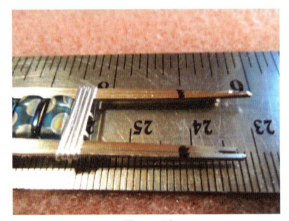

Figure 16

Figure 17

Figure 18

Create the hook for the bracelet. Cut a 4 inch piece of 20-gauge square half-hard wire. Find center and place it in your round-nose pliers, near the back of the pliers (Figure 19). Test fit the bend into the eye of the bracelet (Figure 20). Use the 3rd step on the 3-step pliers and form the bracelet hook. (Figure 21). Mark the hook 3/8" down from the top (Figure 22). Use flat-nose pliers placed at mark and bend wire 90-degrees (Figure 23). Repeat on other side (Figure 24).

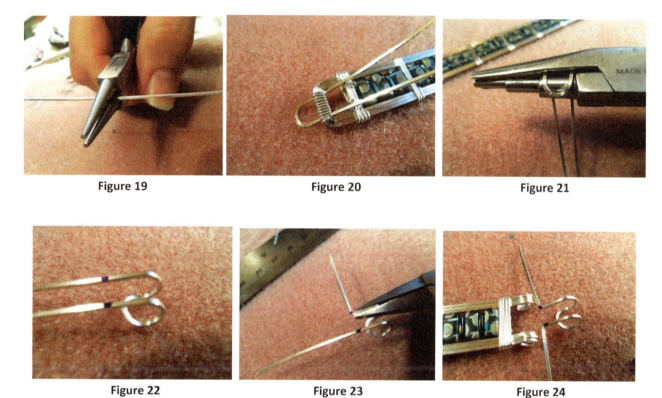

figure 19   figure 20   figure 21

Figure 22   Figure 23   Figure 24

Mark hook wire ½" from the 90-degree bends (Figure 25) and trim wire at marks. Use the 2nd step on the 3-step pliers to form loops on the end of the wire (Figure 26).

Figure 25   Figure 26

Attach hook to bracelet (Figure 27). Form the bracelet (Figure 28).

Figure 27

Figure 28

Completed Channel Bracelet

8

CRYSTAL TEARDROP PENDANT

Tools Required
Flush cutters
Flat-nose pliers
Chain-nose pliers
Round-nose pliers
Ruler
Marker
Tape
Polishing cloth
Nylon jaw pliers

Materials Required
8 in. 10-gauge half-round dead-soft wire
12 in. 20-gauge half-round half-hard wire
Beads of choice

Simply Elegant

Step 1. Make the Pendant Frame

Cut 8 inches of 10-gauge half-round wire and straighten. Find the center and mark (Figure 1). Using nylon jaw pliers, bend the half-round wire horizontally to form the teardrop. Use the corner of the pliers so that the shape will be rounded and not square, since the jaws of the pliers are square (Figures 2 - 4). Keep checking the back of the wire to ensure that it is staying flat as you bend. It will try to cup if you don't keep the wire level as you are bending. If this happens, use the nylon jaw pliers to flatten it.

Figure 1

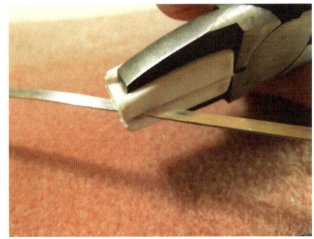

Figure 2

Figure 3

Figure 4

When bending wire, be aware of the type of bend you desire. If you need a very sharp bend, place your fingers next to the pliers when making the bend. If you need a more relaxed or draped bend, keep your fingers further away from the pliers. Get some practice wire and give it a try. It makes a difference.

Continue bending the wire until you have a "U" shape that is 7/8" wide from the outside of the wire (Figure 5). Continue bending the wire past the "U" to more of a teardrop (Figure 6). The outside measurement will now be closer to ¾" wide.

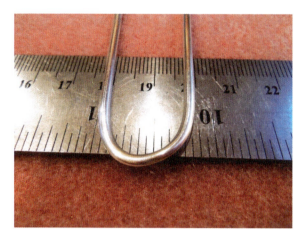
Figure 5

Figure 6

Mark your wire 1.5 inches from the bend on both sides (Figure 7). Use flat-nose pliers and grasp the edge of the half-round wire (Figure 8). Use your fingers very close to the pliers and grasp the wire and bend out (Figure 9). Repeat on other side (Figure 10).

Figure 7

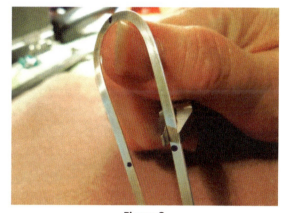
Figure 8

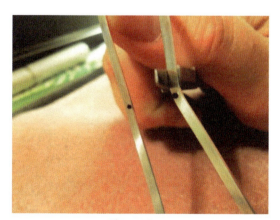
Figure 9

Figure 10

Tape the straight wires together temporarily (Figure 11). Make any adjustment to the fit so that the wires lie next to each other with no gaps.

Remove tape. Cut a 5 inch piece of 20-gauge half-round wire. Place it on the back side of the frame flat side up. Position the small half-round wire, so that 1.5 inches hangs past the teardrop bottom; tape in place (Figure 12).

Figure 11

Figure 12

Take the remaining 7 inches of 20-gauge half-round, make 9 wraps and trim on back (Figure 13).

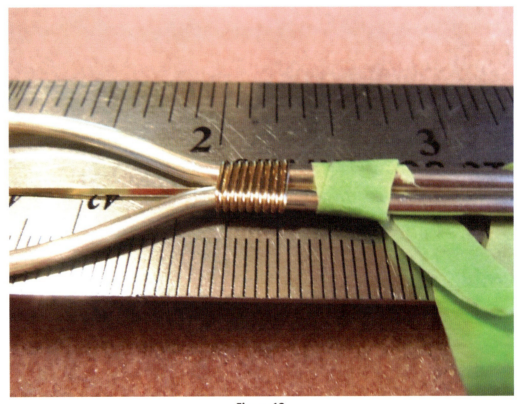

Figure 13

Step 2: Add Beads

Add beads of your choice to middle wire in the teardrop frame (Figure 14).

Figure 14

Use chain-nose pliers to bring the small half-round wire snugly around the bottom of the teardrop (Figure 15). Loop it around a second time, crossing in the back, so that the wire will be even on the front of the pendant (Figure 16). Trim on back.

Figure 15

Figure 16

Lift the small half-round wire up and twist it slightly so that you can begin wrapping with it, ensuring the flat side is against the pendant frame (Figure 17). Make 2 to 3 wraps and trim on back (Figure 18).

Figure 17

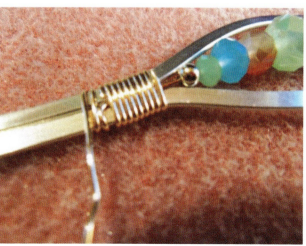

Figure 18

Step 3. Make the Bail

Bend top wires up slightly so that when making the bail, it will be more centered over the top of the pendant (Figure 19). Drape the wire around the round-nose pliers. I'm using the term drape, because I don't want a perfect fit around the pliers (Figure 20).

Figure 19

Figure 20

The half-round wire can be more easily manipulated if you grasp the **end** of the wire in chain-nose pliers. Begin to bring the wire around in a circle that matches the bail that was formed (Figure 21). Continue draping the wire around until the cut end is at the bottom, trimming wire if necessary (Figure 22). Use chain-nose pliers, press the tip of the wire into the loop that was just formed (Figures 23 and 24). Repeat on other side.

Figure 21

Figure 22

Figure 23

Figure 24

Completed Crystal Teardrop Pendant

9

WOVEN BANGLE

Not all Wire Wrapping, but Lots of Fun

Table Vise available at www.Twistsnturns.com

Tools Required
Table Vise and C-clamp
Flush cutters
Flat-nose pliers
Chain-nose pliers
Round-nose pliers
3-step pliers
Ruler
Marker
Tape
Polishing cloth
Nylon jaw pliers

Materials Required
80 in. 20-gauge round dead-soft wire
15 in. 10-gauge half-round dead-soft wire
4 ft. 20-gauge half-round half-hard wire
3 in. 14-gauge round dead-soft wire

Helpful Hints

- Every bend in every wire is important. If you get tired, stop, walk away and come back to it. If you get sloppy when weaving wire, it's really hard to hide.
- Use the center wire that you are weaving over as your control. Keep tension on this wire as you weave. You will actually pull against this wire as you're weaving and this will keep the wires tight and neat.
- Don't run your fingers down the wires every time you work with them. **Dare I say – "Work Harden"?**
- You must weave 1 inch less than the finished length of the bracelet. For a 7 inch bracelet, you must weave 6 inches. The wire that is taped on the end, does not count toward the 6 inches.
- There is a front and back to the weave. If you take it out of the vice, mark the tape with an "X", indicating the front. Make sure you put it back in your vise with the "X" facing you.

Step 1. Prepare Wire and Begin Weaving

Cut eight 10 inch lengths of 20-gauge round dead-soft wire. Tape all together about a ½" from the end. The easiest way that I have found to tape 8 pieces of wire together, side-by-side, is to bundle them up, put the tape on loosely (Figure 1), take flat-nose pliers and press them flat (Figure 2). It seems to work every time.

Figure 1

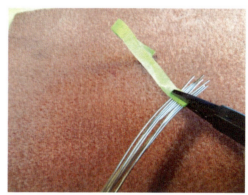

Figure 2

Set up vise: The vise should be clamped to the edge of the table with a C-clamp. As the weave progresses, it will extend past the table edge. Open the vise and put the taped end of the wire in and tighten (Figure 3). Begin weaving by bending each wire at a sharp 90-degree bend at the edge of the vise, one wire coming forward, the next going to the back. Keep alternating until all wires are bent. You should have 4 wires to the front and 4 wires to the back (Figure 4).

Figure 3

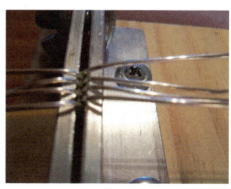

Figure 4

Pick up the first wire on the right-hand side and lay it directly in the center (Figure 5). We will call this the **center** wire.

Alternate bringing the other wires across it. You must keep tension on the center wire to have a good weave.

As you are bending a wire from one side to the other, keep tension on the center wire and actually pull against the wire that is being bent (Figures 6 and 7).

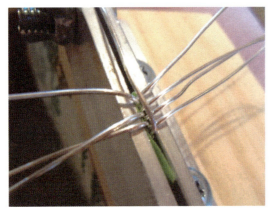

Figure 5

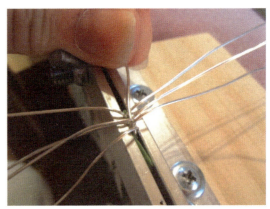

Figure 6

Figure 7

Now you should have 4 wires in the front and 3 in the back, with your center wire out to the left (Figure 8). Bend that center wire sharply to the back. Now you have 4 wires in both the front and back (Figure 9). This is a completed row. You must have an equal number of wires on each side for a row. Weave one more row.

Figure 8

Figure 9

Now open the vise far enough that you can push the woven wires down into the vise, flush with the edge (Figure 10). Tighten the vise.

Figure 10

Weave one row, open the vise, push the weave down flush with the edge, and tighten the vise. Repeat until you have your needed length (Figure 11). The weave will tend to angle to left. Use the nylon jaw pliers to straighten your weave. You can use the pliers to make any small adjustments to get your piece as straight as possible. Trim both ends flush with the weave.

Figure 11

Step 2. The Frame

For a 7 inch bracelet, cut 15 inches of 10-gauge half-round dead-soft wire and straighten. Find the center and mark (Figure 12).

Figure 12

Use nylon jaw pliers to bend the half-round wire horizontally to form the frame (Figure 13). Use the corner of the pliers so that the shape will be rounded, and not square, since the jaws of the pliers are square (Figure 14). Keep checking the back of the wire to ensure that it is staying flat as you bend. It will try to cup, if you don't keep the wire level as you are bending. If this happens, use the nylon jaw pliers to flatten it (Figure 15). Keep bending until the frame fits your weave (Figure 16).

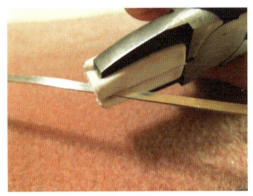

Figure 13

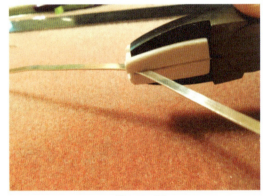

Figure 14

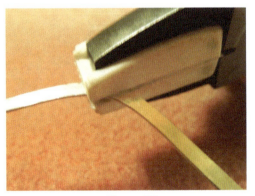

Figure 15

Figure 16

Tape frame around the weave. Use 12 inches of 20-gauge half-round and start wrapping by leaving a long tail that can be wrapped around the single side (Figure 17). This will keep the wrapping wire from slipping. After 9 or 10 wraps, wrap the remainder twice around the opposite side (Figure 18). DO NOT press your wraps with flat nose pliers. The imprint of the weave will dent the wraps. Wrap opposite end with another 12 inch piece of half round wire.

Figure 17

Figure 18

After both ends are wrapped, measure the distance between the wraps, and divide by 2. Use this number to measure from one end to find the center of your bracelet, and mark it (Figure 19). Cut 8 inches of 20-gauge half-round wire for the center wraps. The easiest way to wrap at a center point is to bend the half-round wire in half and wrap to each end (Figure 20).

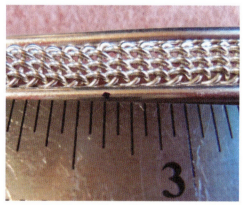

Figure 19

Figure 20

The nylon pliers assist in keeping the frame wire from overlapping your weave, while you are making the center wraps (Figure 21). Leave enough wire to secure the cut ends by wrapping twice on opposite sides of the frame (Figure 22).

Figure 21

Figure 22

Measure the distance between the center wrap and the end wrap, and divide by 2 (Figure 23). Use this number to measure from the center and make your last 2 sets of wraps on each side of center using 8 inches on each wrap (Figure 24).

Figure 23

Figure 24

Step 3. The Hook

Bend the end wires up slightly, measure ½" from your wraps, and trim (Figure 25). Use the 2nd step on the 3-step pliers and make the loops to receive your hook (Figure 26). Bend wires to the back.

Figure 25

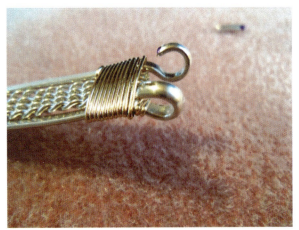
Figure 26

Cut 3 inches of 14-gauge dead-soft wire for the hook. Find middle, and bend wire in half. Press wire closer, but not completely closed (refer to the hook instructions in the "Basics" section, page 4). Form hook using the 2nd step on the 3-step pliers (Figure 27). Mark wire ½" from the top of the hook (Figure 28).

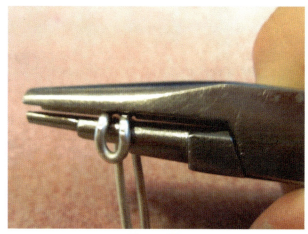
Figure 27

Figure 28

Use flat-nose pliers to grasp the wires as shown (Figure 29). Bend wires out 90-degrees to the side (Figure 30).

Figure 29

Figure 30

Trim wires, if necessary to ½" past the last bend (Figure 31). If you used exactly 3 inches of wire, you shouldn't have to trim. Use the 2nd step on 3-step pliers to form loops (Figure 32). Attach hook to bracelet (Figure 33).

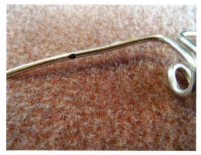
Figure 31

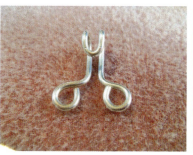
Figure 32

Figure 33

Completed Woven Bangle

10

Double Loop Cabochon Wrap

Cabochon Wrap with a Twist

Tools Required
Flush cutters
Flat-nose pliers
Chain-nose pliers
Round-nose pliers
3-step pliers
Ruler
Marker
Tape
Polishing cloth

Materials Required
Oval cabochon
3 ft. of 22-gauge square dead-soft wire
10 in. of 22-gauge half-round half-hard wire

The material list is for 1 wrapped cabochon. The amount of material listed is suitable for up to a 30 x 22mm cabochon. I originally designed this to be added to a beaded project, worn to the side. I have since used this as a stand-alone pendant, adding a snap bail, and used the bottom loop for beaded tassels. I have increased the size of the loops at the top and made a hinged bracelet. Pictured is very small cabochons linked together to form a bracelet. Have fun deciding how you would like to use your double-loop cabochon.

Step 1. Prepare Your Wire

Cut six 6 inch pieces of 22-gauge dead-soft square wire, and straighten. Make 2 groups with 3 wires each. Mark center of each wire. Tape the wire of each group at 1 inch both sides of center (Figure 1). Using the 1st step on 3-step pliers, or the very end of round-nose pliers, form loops at the center of both sets of wires (Figures 2 – 4).

Figure 1

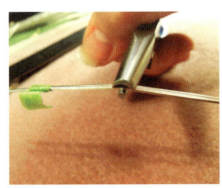
Figure 2

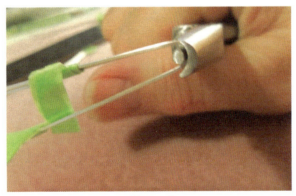
Figure 3

Figure 4

Cut 4 inches of half-round wire. Make a bend at the end. Insert the bent end into the loop. Insert the chain-nose pliers into the loop, holding the half-round wire (Figure 5). Make 4 wraps around the group of wires. Trim end on the outside of wire, and trim the end in the loop as close as possible (Figure 6). Repeat on 2nd set.

Figure 5

Figure 6

Separate the wires directly below the wraps. Start shaping the wires along the top and side of your cabochon (Figure 7). Remove the tape and fan out the wires (Figure 8). Repeat with 2nd set. Bring the sets together and interlace the wires (Figure 9). Tape the sides in 2 places, leaving the center open so that wraps can be made (Figure 10).

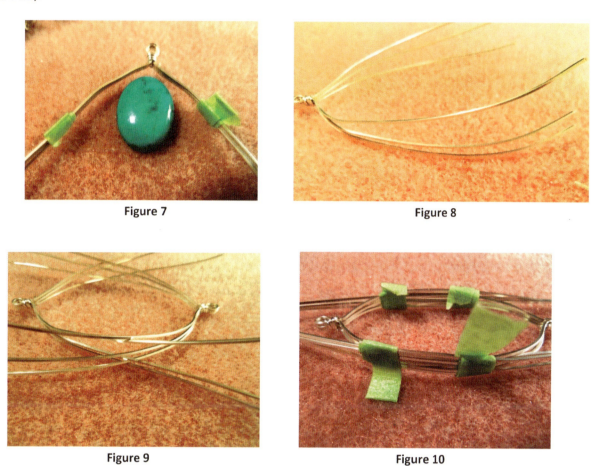

Figure 7

Figure 8

Figure 9

Figure 10

Use half round wire and make 3 wraps on each side (Figure 11). It is very important that you do not make these wraps tight. The square wires need to move freely within them.

Figure 11

Remove tape and start pulling the wires on each side alternating back and forth until you have a good fit for the cabochon (Figures 12 and 13).

Figure 12

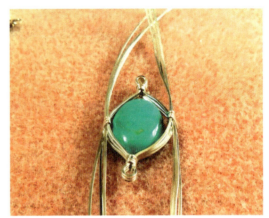
Figure 13

Begin securing the cabochon by making bends on the front wires (Figure 14). *See Ammonite Pendant, page 12, for more photos.* Once all 4 bends have been made on the front, set the cabochon in the frame and make the same bends on the back (Figure 15). Some of the wires may need to be adjusted once the stone is in (Figure 16). The wires are still not secure. The best way to secure them is to pull them snug when they are used to embellish the piece (Figure 17).

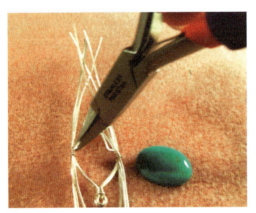
Figure 14

Figure 15

Figure 16

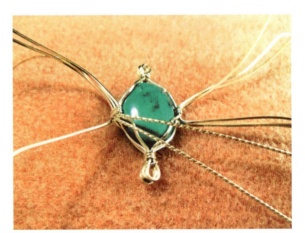
Figure 17

The top and bottom loops have 3 wires. In the bracelet that I am making, I have no need for all three, so I am using my flat-nose pliers to fold down the front and back loops (Figure 18). Continue using each piece of wire as an embellishment. The wires can be used on the front, back or sides (Figure 19 - 21).

Figure 18

Figure 19

Figure 20

Figure 21

Completed Double Loop Cabochon

ABOUT THE AUTHOR

Since taking my first wire wrap jewelry class in 2003 with Bobbie Brown, I was immediately hooked on the many facets of jewelry design. I continued my education at William Holland lapidary school with classes in advanced wire wrap design, silver smith techniques and received my certification in Precious Metal Clay. I continue to take classes in new areas such as enameling and bead weaving. I love to learn new things, but my first love will always be wire wrap design.

I am inspired by traditional wire wrap pieces and my work leans to more traditional designs. I love to use natural stones in my work and I feel the wire should enhance the piece, not overpower it.

In my accounting profession, I enjoy my position as a trainer. So it was a natural progression to move from creating to instructing. I began teaching at local bead stores in Florida and Georgia in 2006. In 2007, I started teaching at both the Down the Street and the Intergalactic Bead Shows. I can also be found teaching at Mandarin High School in their Community Education program.

My newest venture is with my business partner, Jenny Shibona of Mad Chiwawa Designs. We have an annual retreat called The Great Bead Escape Retreat. We have over 10 instructors with us to give our attendees their choice of classes in over 15 different jewelry disciplines. You can read more about it at www.thegreatbeadescaperetreats.com.

Made in the USA
Charleston, SC
27 August 2015